Things I Don't Want to Think About, but Sometimes do

Abigail Murphy

BookLeaf Publishing
India | USA | UK

Presentation by *BookLeaf Publishing*

Web: www.bookleafpub.com

E-mail: info@bookleafpub.com

ISBN: 978-93-5744-338-8

First edition 2022

DEDICATION

To a younger me

ACKNOWLEDGEMENT

To my parents and my best friend, Nicole--it was a hard year, but you were always here.

PREFACE

The poems in my collection are all a snapshot of what I think about when I can't fall asleep, or when I wake up in the morning and there's only one thing on my mind. They're thoughts I wish I sometimes didn't have, but also the thoughts the make me me, because they've stemmed from my unique walk through life and they've given me the obstacles that I've overcome. While they're deeply personal, I think they're fairly universal, and by sharing them I hope I can lessen the world's collective burden, if just by a little.

my life, unfeeling

Harsh lit lamps and soft warm hues
Lemon prints and I love yous
Window panes and noisy trains
And people going home.

Metal shades and morning light
Barren walls and three missed calls
I am unwell, I am unwell
I hope that you can’t tell.

My skin is melting, the walls are falling
How are you today?
My mind is crying, I swear I’m trying
How are you okay?

Cheesy eggs and toaster lines
Here we are again.
Victorian novels, midterms, finals
I’m not sure who’s my friend.

Lime green walls and silent halls,
And someone I thought I knew
Plaster peeling, my life, unfeeling
I wish this wasn’t true.

little lives

Sometimes all I see is me,
Living life through a telescope.
A kaleidoscope of shapes and sounds
That don't truly belong to me.

Sometimes all I see is darkness,
Smoke billowing over waves.
Little kids playing, waiting for the bus
Suddenly enveloped by night, by dust.

I try to tell her this isn't me,
And all she does is fix me.
All she does is stitch me up
With a thread that doesn't fit me.

Now I see me on the train,
Turtle neck sweater, folded hands.
I see me pondering the meaning of life,
The meaning of all these little lives.

dandelion seed

I can feel my top half but I'm not sure where the
bottom half went,
Like I'm buried in the sand and just a head and
two arms.
Maybe someone made a sidewalk out of me,
a bridge between the sky and the ground
Because I can see what is happening above me,
I just can't see down.

Someone is tying a string around my waist
Because now I can't feel my legs
and I'm in a room with many doors
But I can't find a single key

I feel like a buoy, watching the tides change
around me
Chained where I am, moving but going nowhere.
Sometimes I stay above the waves, but
sometimes I lay on the sand
Wishing and waiting for something to lift me up
off the ground.

I’m a dandelion seed walking in the wind:
I know I have meaning to someone, somewhere,
I’m just not sure who and I’m just not sure
where.
I am the clothes on my bedroom floor,
the cards that slip away from the perfect shuffle,
because all of those things belong somewhere
They just seem to have forgotten where.

I crave intimacy, they crave sex

As a woman, the world assumes certain rights to me: guys, for example, see me for the size of my features. I know when I walk down the street they don't notice my blue eyes, like I hope, instead they size me up to see if my measurements deserve their time. They slip my shirt over my head, then put it back on when they're done, they stick their fingers in me as if the life-giving parts of me are made for them, not for me. I crave intimacy, they crave sex–yes, there's a difference but am I the only one who thinks so? I should not have to fear rejection for denying them access, but what if at the end they suddenly lose interest? I wish we had just talked for four hours and went our separate ways, I wish we had just talked that day and were still talking today.

things I don't want to think about, but sometimes do

I told you I wasn't mad at you, but I now know that isn't true. I'm so mad I can barely look at your street sign, and when I pass your model of car I pass it in the other lane, quickly. I'm so mad that you broke my heart because you don't deserve to break my heart, you don't deserve another ounce of thought but then again maybe you do. You told me you that loved me and then the next night you didn't; all the sudden you changed it to past tense and I thought to myself, wait a second, when did that happen? Because sure, I didn't want to marry you, and sure we didn't make each other laugh, but you made me happy, okay, I don't know what to say. You made me really happy and I really wanted to stay. You made me happy because you took me to the Open, you met my friends and let me believe you'd see them again like you'd said. You'll never see them again and I get it, okay,

I’m not mad I’m not the one for you because you’re not the one for me. I knew that before you did, before you told me you loved me three weeks in. I’m mad that you gave me hope, at a time when I really needed it–you pretended to piece life

you were neither

Sometimes I wonder
whether it'd be better
if I never knew you;
It may save me
centuries of heartache
But then I guess I'd never know
you, or the way you feel
Or what it is to cry at the sight of someone.
What it is to cradle your head in my arms
and know that we were keeping each other
alive.

I hate how tight
I was under your grasp
(and am still)
And the fact that you never knew how much I
loved you.
I hate that I couldn't fix you
And the fact that you left me broken.
I hate that you didn't text me on my birthday
And I hate that we're not friends.
I hate that you don't need me
And that I probably don't need you.

Sometimes (often) I think about you
About those nights you were two different people,
About those nights you looked me in the eye
And there was nothing in your eyes.
Other times I think about you
Sitting across from me at the Blue Colony diner
Or across from me in a blue car
Singing to Biggie Smalls.
I hate to be honest,
But I have to be honest.
Do you know what happened?
Do you know what happened.

Sometimes I think about me, and how I didn't have a clue
Or maybe I did, but I certainly didn't want to
Leave, or even stay
Or admit that you were wrong,
I didn't want to say
That I made a big mistake.
I used to think it was a beautiful mess
But now I think it's just a mess.
And everytime I try to categorize you
With labels of good or bad
I draw a blank and realize
That maybe you were neither.

I know it's stupid

I know it's stupid, you don't have to tell me that,
Okay?
I know it's stupid
To think about someone
More than once a day

I know it's stupid to think about it
Like it's the only thing making me happy
But honestly these days, it really is
The only thing making me happy

I know it's stupid to think about it
In general, or even at all.
I know it is, because I know he's not
But that's never stopped me before.

I know it's stupid, but is it really
to think about green lights and fish tanks,
Kitchen islands and borrowed wine?
Is it so bad to think about shag carpet, dirty bathrooms,
And losing track of time?

Will I have a window, will I have a plant?

I walked into Dr. Berk's office and he made some sort of joke, and I thought here is a man in the middle of saving lifes and he still retains the ability to joke. That's when I realized maybe it's not the ability to joke, but rather the affinity to–it's the fact that Dr. Berk goes to a job everyday, one that energizes him enough to have a sense of humor at the end of the day. I got scared all the sudden, and sad, because I wondered if I would ever find a job like that. I wondered if one day I'd have my own office, one with my own desk and my own plant and my own window that looks over the parking lot. I wondered if one day I'd be able to love what I'm doing, because right now I don't love what I'm doing, at least fully. It's just that I dropped out of college (I didn't mean to) and now I'm a secretary, and everything just feels so far out of reach at this point. It's like I can see the edge of the horizon, the one I'm trying to reach, but I have no way of getting there and no idea how long it will be.

They tell me it's okay, and I know that it will be, but I have these standards for myself that I just need to meet.

dear me

I think it's funny that you don't know half of
what you will know
not funny in the way of ha ha
but funny in the way of hmm, isn't life funny.
I wonder why you always have to correct
yourself when speaking
or not correct, so much as clarify
as if the worst thing in the world is to not be
clear.
Anyways it's weird, don't you think
that every week you've lived is made up
of the same number of hours, same number
of days. The same monday that becomes tuesday
becomes wednesday becomes thursday
all too fast until the day you die
And then there are no more days.

I like the way you live your life like a movie;
I think about the main characters
And the minor ones too.
I think about Katie and how she
eats the heel of the bread
I think about Chrissy and how she

said you'd have two boys and a girl.
You'd probably be my favorite character,
but not for reasons you'd expect.
It wouldn't be because you are me
but because of the way you write things down:
A quote from pinterest
in the waiting room of a meeting
a quote from a song
of a band you've never heard.
The way you look at leaves
and realize they are heart shaped,
The way you see a red toyota
and think of the boy that writes.

If I was watching you in a movie
I'd think you're pretty funny.
I'd laugh when you followed him
out of the train like that
and tell you to probably just say something,
if you felt like that.
I'd laugh at how you wish your days away,
Wanting to be in the future
or in the past.

I looked at a grocery receipt today
And also thought of you.
It said Modern Market,

Bronx New York. seventy-six dollars.
I held it in my hand and
Pictured you finding it years later,
Maybe in your house with your kids or your husband.
You'd think about today:
About the air and the birds,
The people on the street,
And ally looking for zucchini.

manchester by the sea

They made a movie about this town
Which is funny, because my mom grew up here
And it's not much different from other towns
Other than that it's the one place
I feel free.

On sunday I had a mental breakdown
Which actually is not new.
What was new was the magnitude
Of this attack
Which left me flooded with tears
And devoid of breath.
Normally I keep my suffering to myself
(I am my most comforting presence)
But this time I was busy losing it
So I called out to my mom.

All I said was "Mom"
And she already knew something was wrong
She climbed in my bed and rubbed my back
And told me I would be okay
what I really needed, though, was something else
What I really needed was

The sea: boats in the harbor on a cloudy day
And the smell of salt air through my lungs.
I'm going to manchester, I said, but my mom
said
No, not like that.
She hates when I drive when I'm upset,
though I've gotten quite good at it.

I'll go with you, she said, but I didn't want to
bother her.
No, no, she said. We'll go. Let's go.
So we got in my highlander and played Colbie
Calliet
And at the rest stop my mom said the boy was
looking at me.
We passed the cemetery, and the ice cream shop,
then made it to the harbor
We parked the car and sat on the bench
And simply looked out on the water
It was foggy out, and the water was still,
Silver like liquid mercury.
The boats sat silent, chained to their buoys,
facing the direction of the sea.
I followed their gaze and sat just as silent,
Wishing I could be like them.
Out for the season, chained to something other
than myself
just sitting, silent, watching the sea.

home

If I close my eyes I can see it: my father sitting on the stonewall in the dimming light of the sun, my dog lapping around in circles while my mother watches contentedly from the kitchen window. I can smell the scent of pork rolling steadily out of the smoker, and it smells like sunday afternoon in the middle of october. Through the leaves of the trees is the tiger-striped sky, the pink and purple and orange that render me speechless, everytime. The wind carries the voices of my neighbors: playing basketball or pleading their dog to come in, and the smoke of their bonfire drifts casually to our yard. My bones ache with the coldness of late fall, early winter, and the air smells tight, the way it smells before it snows. Once the sun sets, the stars will settle in, and unlike in the city I can see the big dipper. After a while we'll go inside, and watch football for the rest of the night--I can hear the dull roar of a sports announcer as I drift intentionally off to sleep. At the end of the night when my mother shakes me awake, I will pretend not to hear her, or tell them to stay five more minutes.

spectacle pond

I live in a small town and all my life
I hated that.
I hated that I could drive from one side to the other
In under ten minutes
And list all the people I liked
On only one hand.

When I moved away I said I was from Boston
But I'm not. I'm from Littleton.
Littleton is a little-town, not named for its size.
it's home of the nation's most-visited gas station
off route 495.
We used to have four Dunkin Donuts, but now
I think it's just three.
We have two different grocery stores
And seven different farms.

It's how it always goes:
When you're away from something you learn to love it
And absence makes the heart grow fonder
But so does presence, too.
I've never done this, but I'm starting to

Love my little town.
The longer I stay here, on this silent road,
Driving on these winding roads.

There's a particular place I'm thinking of,
Right off route 119
That you'll hit if you're heading away from
town
Towards Johnson's, where I worked.
It's not a place, so much as a view
Of the sunset over spectacle pond

It's nothing special, and it's nothing new
But there's something about the water
and the train tracks and the power lines and
the trees and the road and the sky
That make me think that I am full
And this is all I'll ever need.

train tracks make me sad

Train tracks make me sad, here's why:
They're always on the run.
They're always on the run
It's just that
No one knows what from

Train tracks outside my window
Made me think of life
Made me think of the meaning of it
Or maybe the lack thereof

Train tracks make me want to slip
Unnoticeably into space
They make me want to fall asleep
To forget the music I've yet to face.

Train tracks make me sad, here's why
I always have been sad.
I always wanted to leave that town
The train was my only out.

One afternoon I ran away
A took a train up north
I wasn't alive that day,

I swear, just a bundle of cells heading north.

the best thing I could have done

You asked me to come to the graduation
Of a school I will not graduate from
You told me it'd mean so much to you
If I were just to come

You told me lots of things, of course
Like how I'm your best friend
You told me lots of things, like how
I shouldn't just pretend

You make me feel in trouble, like
I've done something wrong in class
You make me feel like I'm hiding things.
I thought this was going to last

You tell me it'd be so special for you
For me to come and support
But I'm having trouble thinking that
On that day I'd be a good sport

Because I dropped out of college,
And I'm fine with that, really,
But all this push is coming to shove.
It's making me think that in reality, really
This is the best thing I could have done.

someday I'll love abby

Someday I'll love abby
the way my mother claims she does
I'll love all the things
People love about
even if they're the things I hate.
Maybe someday I'll make the jokes I keep to myself,
or learn to speak my mind.
Maybe someday I'll learn to say something,
Or learn that I have something to say.

Sometimes I picture my own funeral,
Of all the people in the back of a church.
I think about them wiping their tears
And making remarks about how kind I was.
I wonder how many people would come?
To my funeral.
And if the magnitude of their hurt
Would measure up to my standards.
Isn't that selfish, though?
To want people to want me.
Or how about this:
do you think it's selfish--or necessary--
for me to want me?

This morning my parents discussed football
with my brother
while I was making waffles
at the counter.
All of the sudden,
I made a perfect waffle, and I
held it up to show my mother.
But she wasn't even looking, and
I wondered, then,iIs it true?
That parents do have favorites,
and that some people just don't belong?
Neither at home, nor anywhere,
but if there's no home, then what is there?

In small windows I see myself,
like between the stitches of a
Ralph Lauren sweater.
or between the lines
of a Roger Reeves poem, and that's when I think
does there have to be more to life
than chasing after the things you love,
until you breathe the music that moves you
and speak the poetry that makes you cry,
until all of a sudden what you love
stops representing you
And simply
becomes you?

triangle street

One day you'll wake up and realize it wasn't them, after all–it never was and it never will be. You'll wake up one day after crying yourself to sleep and realize that you're alone, yes still, but since when was that a bad thing? Since when did we convince ourselves that to strike out was misery, that to be alone was to be alone forever? Who said that cheap dates and bad sex were better than wine glasses, laughter, and The Parent Trap? I'd rather be alone than in bad company (we can all agree), but why can't I remember that when a man throws himself at my feet? I hate that I define my worth by the last time I kissed someone; after all, who knows that except me and him? I think it goes back to a long line of forgetting, a century of overlooking and as a result, overcompensating. It goes back to not knowing myself (the real me), deep down–it goes back to getting to know myself by getting to know others. It goes back to the fact that if you aren't desirable, you aren't desired, and if you aren't desired, you forfeit the right to desire others.

But one day you'll drive past Triangle Street and you won't feel the need to tell him, you won't want to be wanted by him because you're already wanted by you. Soon enough you'll want him, but not because you need him; you'll want him because he's perfect for you and you can't picture your life without him. You'll stop making sacrifices (big ones or small) because you'll realize that your happiness is the most valuable thing of all. And that's when you're in the car, singing at your best, sunshine on your face and you don't care if they see you dancing.

you'll thank god

Some time soon, the sun will shine
Though it might not be today.
It might not be tomorrow,
and it will not last forever.

Some time soon, you'll wake up happy
And for no reason at all
Except the fact that maybe it's raining
And you've always loved the rain.

Some time soon you'll shower and shave
And it won't take a day off your life
Some time soon you'll dry your hair
And wear pants that fit just right

Some time soon might not come soon at all
No, it might be quite a while
It might leave as soon as it comes (it often does)
But when it shines it will be at sunset.

And when you look you'll be grateful,
And maybe even a little sad
You'll thank god for putting
Something so beautiful in your backyard.

be brave

Lately I've had dreams about my grandfather
The one who died when I was eight
I feel as if I know him well
Though I never got to know him, not well

I know that he liked music,
And I know he sang in church
I know that he was funny,
He made my mother laugh

His hair was white and curly,
That much, I remember.
His smile was a beam of light
It froze perfectly in time.

In my dreams he makes my day
I'm so happy to see him, I could cry
Yet all the sudden he runs away
Again, I am alone.

My mother says he loved me a lot
And used to ask, where's that little girl
I remember us sitting on the couch one day
I remember the top of the stairs

I remember your birthday party
What was it, eighty five?
I remember brick walls and paper decor
And a nurse pushing you through the door

I carry your photo around with me
Though I swear, we've never really talked
By the time i could say your name
You'd long forgotten mine

I still feel like we're friends, somehow
And i know you would be proud
You used to tell my mother, "be brave"
I hope lately I've been brave.

www.ingramcontent.com/pod-product-compliance
Lightning Source LLC
Chambersburg PA
CBHW051749130826
49812CB00033B/1064
9789357443388